For the meek

Simon Haines

Rosewood Press 2021

ISBN 978-1-7398759-0-9

Contents

Poetry today

In our world of harsh reality
there's no justification for poetry.
That may be sad, but you can't deny it
try justifying your favourite poet.
I mean, who now has the
time to stand and stare
at pretty words that try to snare
us with their rhymes, their scanning twee
except poor fantasists like me?

For the meek

We wonder how we fit in the world.
The stories they tell us are not true.
Expect repression to follow the coup.
Their patterned flags are being unfurled.
Abusive threats and insults hurled
at those who do not join the queue,
whether the many or the few.
The meek will not inherit the earth.

Yet!

Stuff the cat sent

I've told you before I'm going deaf,
confusing letters like S and F.
It's sometimes sad and sometimes funny.
It can be quite dangerous related to money.

My daughter rang the other day
for a DIY chat, and just to say
she was bored with her job and wanted to move,
she hoped that I'd listen and not disapprove.

"Fine by me," I said. "Why should I mind?
Look at the job ads - see what you can find."
Now her boyfriend's decided he wants to move too.
He's fed up with his old job and wants something new.

"At the moment his work is too far from home,
The drive can be tricky; he travels alone."
"Is that his main reason?" I asked quite surprised.
"No, there's one much more serious," she calmly replied.

"His job's near the docks in Felixstowe,
That's a free port in Suffolk, you probably know."
"What's wrong with that?" I asked with a smile.
"He prefers Essex – it suits his lifestyle."

"But quite apart from that," she said
"There's another thing messing with his head
It's something he's trying very hard to prevent:
He's frightened of catching the stuff the cat sent."

"What stuff did the cat send?" I naively inquired.
"Was it something his workplace actually required?"
My daughter laughed at me quite disbelieving.
"No, cats aren't involved in his reason for leaving."

It was then that she realized my stupid confusion
Was because of my deafness and not an illusion
"It's nothing to do with stuff the cat sent
He's trying not to catch the Suffolk accent."

Toblerone boy

Is that my son at the self-checkout,
the boy with the large Toblerone,
in worn down shoes and a tatty coat,
Mumbling sadly into his phone?

They didn't tell me he'd lost his job
as a government consultant,
advising ministers on trade and finance,
inflation and interest rates.

He could be mine, he could be his.
The dates are inconclusive.
I saw him when just a few months old -
a weakling, meek and helpless.

The Toblerone's real, but he's not a boy;
he's a man of forty-nine,
still deeply involved in trade and finance,
which means he can't be mine.

Guardian of the Galaxy

According to my grandson Stanley
I'm a Guardian of the Galaxy,
together with himself and Max the cat
and the grandma he calls Nanny.

I'm trying hard to discover
if it's something I've already done
or a future thing I'm yet to do:
a daring deed or something fun.

Never thought I could be a guardian
of anything, let alone a galaxy.
unless it's the chocolate I kept for myself
and ate – oh what depravity!

There's nothing in my past I've done
to merit such regard.
I'm not a superhero, me,
I'm no one's bodyguard.

I'd like to think I'll rid the world
one day, of fascist beasts -
like Ronald Chump or Doris Johns
and other noxious priests.

So thank you Stanley for thinking of me
as a Guardian of the Galaxy,
but you are young, so it's now your job
to ensure the world stays free.

Bird at Sizewell

It looked straight at me - a static sentinel,
standing in the cool spring sun, on spikey yellow gorse.
Could it see me? Could it hear me?
Hard to tell, with its song so sweet.

I whipped out my phone, chose video to catch the song
and any hasty move. Surely it would fly away, but No!
It stared directly at me into my camera lens.
for thirty seconds singing - not moving, just the song.

I stopped the film, put down my phone;
it wasn't there – it must have flown.
It was smaller than a starling, but larger than a robin.
It could have been a linnet or perhaps a type of finch.

I sent my little video to a keen bird-watcher friend -
an expert on African species, he said he wasn't sure.
But when I told him I had seen it on a gorse bush by the coast,
he guessed it was a stonechat or a linnet.

A linnet is what I'd like it to be -
I'll watch my film occasionally,
I'll always wonder if it saw or heard me
as it stood on the gorse by the sea.

Middle lane thoughts

It was driving along on the inside lane
sounding more like a military plane.
It was long and shiny and very dark.
The driver in black was a mean-looking shark.

I thought no more of it as I sang along,
in the middle lane to a cheesy song.
Then I looked in my mirror; it was now quite near:
A sleek new hearse, it filled me with fear.

I tried to keep calm, but it got much closer.
I thought of death and things much grosser.
I mean, can you think of anything worse
than being undertaken by an empty hearse?

Locusts will thrive

Daffodils arrive before Christmas,
roses bloom for New Year,
vineyards thrive on our hillsides
so my wine won't be so dear.

Well...
That's one effect of climate change,
but there's a more disturbing flip-side:
flooding and menacing heatwaves
causing ruin and death worldwide.
With the ice cap and glaciers melting,
and sea levels rising at speed,
low-lying countries may soon disappear
leaving millions of souls in need
of shelter and food and security -
will we help them or turn them away?
Will we close our borders and sink their boats
as they plead for a chance to stay?

And...
Wildlife won't fare any better
if their habitats disappear.
As temperatures and rainfalls rise,
they'll migrate for food elsewhere.
Some will die in the process
of their frantic attempt to survive;
others will exploit the chaos -
locusts, for example, will thrive.
They'll swarm to destroy the crops
others need to stay alive.

But...
Daffodils arrive before Christmas,
roses bloom for new year,
vineyards thrive on our hillsides
so my wine won't be so dear.

The office-next-door

As our drone hovered over the office-next-door,
was it sensed by their CEE-CEE-TEE-VEE?
Did they relay a message to MI5?
Would special branch dash to the scene?

Our drone was deadly efficient
in its casing of sparkling blue,
but the battery died over the office-next-door,
so it crashed there and lay in full view.

But no-one rushed from the office-next-door.
Perhaps nobody heard the drone fall.
We waited for several minutes,
then slyly peeped over the wall.

The blue drone lay there in the open,
its tiny light flashing bright green.
But GCHQ in the office-next-door
were all glued to their little square screens.

The secret agents in the office-next-door
all left their positions at five.
We waited until they'd locked all their doors,
but their security lights came alive.

Our drone still lay there blinking,
on the path of the office-next-door.
Did their lights have security cameras?
Would they know if we broke the law?

Donning a black balaclava,
I scaled the wall of the office-next-door.
No alarms were set off - Thank goodness!
In fact nothing happened at all.

In the distance I heard a police siren.
It came near, then faded away.
I picked up the drone and I legged it,
lived to spy another day.

Your space flight

How long would you get to spend in space
if the length of your flight depended
on the extent of the wealth you owned?

Jeff Bezos, you know, Amazon man,
is worth two-o-five billion dollars -
his flight lasted ten minutes.

Now check your bank balance.
What are you worth?
How long would your space flight last?

Hither, thither and whither

Hither, *thither* and *whither* are
archaic slash literary, they say.
Why don't we resurrect them,
and use them every day?

Now of course *here*, *there* and *where*
are employed, instead of these,
but they convey no movement -
they're as still as stones or trees.

Hence, *thence* and *whence*
are similarly out of style.
I'm going to use them when I can
Just to make some people smile.

My granddad said *yon* and *yonder*.
Yon bugger a favourite expression
of his to mean that chap over there,
without a hint of aggression.

He also said *thou*, *thy* and *thine* -
singulars of *you*, *your* and *yours*.
But we rarely hear any of these nowadays.
They're Amazon rainforest words.

I'm not going to mention *henceforth*,
thenceforth, or even *whenceforth*,
because they'd mess my scansion up
And it'd be completely impossible to find a rhyme for *whenceforth*.

Feeding the birds

During our long cold winters
we're urged to feed the birds.
It used to be on bacon rind
and crusts from children's toast.

Now the supermarkets sell us
sacks of seeds and balls of fat
to put in special feeders
and hang from garden trees.

I didn't have much luck last year.
My seeds reduced quite slowly,
and, victims of the elements,
my balls of fat turned crumbly.

This year the bird food's going quite quickly
I've hung feeders from our walls.
Goldfinches gorge on the dangling seeds.
There are tits on my fat balls.

Heroes

Elvis, the King, sang *Heartbreak Hotel*,
but did he grow spuds in his garden?

Genet, gay thief, wrote four novels and five plays,
but could he play scottisches on the bagpipes?

Ornette played *European Echoes* on his saxophone,
but did he make hot curries for his friends?

Piazzolla's bandoneon set the tango world alight,
but did he decorate the outside of his house?

Monk played *Round Midnight* on the shiny grand piano,
but was he any good at doing crosswords?

Befuddled fish

Have you noticed that the fishes
in your river or your stream
can't concentrate on anything,
they're swimming in a dream?

Are the trout a little dopey?
Are the minnows rather slow?
Are the perch and pike dim-witted?
Do the chub have vertigo?

Well, the answer is quite simple:
it's to do with treated waste
which leaks into our rivers,
and spreads a nasty taste.

How does this treated waste
affect our scaly friends?
What is it in the water
that drives them round the bend?

It's all of us who are to blame
if we're feeling tired 'n stressed
and taking daily Prozac
to stop being so depressed.

It's the Prozac in the waste we flush
that gets into the fish,
and makes them feel less lively
and easier to squish.

Are the trout a little dopey?
Are the minnows rather slow?
Are the perch and pike dim-witted?
Do the chub have vertigo?

Prozak in rivers 'impairs fish and puts them at risk' (The i 10/02/21)

May to October

Late on a May evening
He walked her home.
They stumbled up a grassy bank
She said "I love you."

Two weeks later going upstairs,
she looked down at him
with such sad eyes,
and said "I'll hurt you."

A few months later in September
after a summer of separation,
her loving eyes looked up at him;
she said "I'm overwhelmed."

She acted in a college play;
He helped her with the words.
By October it was over -
she said, "Sorry, but I warned you."

Your call is important to us

Good afternoon. Thank you for calling. We are experiencing an abnormally high volume of calls at present...
>*How high? How many calls?*

We apologise that you are still waiting. Please continue to hold and an adviser will answer your call shortly.
>*How shortly?*

Your call is important to us.
>*How important?*

All our advisers are currently dealing with other customers.
>*How many advisers do you have?*

All our calls are recorded for training and quality purposes.
>*How many advisers have you fired as a result of this system?*

You are now being placed in a queue.

You are number S-E-V-E-N-T-E-E-N.

> Little darling, it's been a long cold lonely winter
> Little darling, it seems like years since it's been here
> Here comes the sun do, do, do
> Here comes the sun
> And I say it's all right

Hello, how can I help you this morning?
>*It's afternoon now.*

I'm so sorry. Have you been waiting long?
>*Only fifty minutes.*

That's better than yesterday.
>*Oh, that's alright then.*

Could I have you full name please?
>*Yes, it's Joe Harris.*

Brilliant. Is that Jo with an E?
>*Yes*

Brilliant. And could you tell me your postcode and house number?"
>*Yes. It's postcode IP7 5XU, number 14*

Brilliant. And how can I help this morning, Joe?
>*I just need to update my motor insurance policy.*

Brilliant. Could I take your policy number?
>*MO-PL-76591.*

Brilliant. I'm just loading your details.
>*Thank you.*
You're welcome. I'll just have to pop you on hold for a moment.
Can you bear with me?
>*Sure.*
Brilliant. Thank you.

>Little darling, it's been a long cold lonely winter
>Little darling, it seems like years since it's been here
>Here comes the sun do, do, do
>Here comes the sun
>And I say it's all right

Sorry for the delay.
>*No worries.*
I can see here that your policy has updated automatically, so you don't need to do anything now.
>*Oh really?– Okay.*
Is there anything else I can help you with today?
>*Just a moment. Let me think. .... No there's nothing*
Brilliant. Thank you. Now you have a nice day.

Back in the day

Correct me if I'm wrong, but back in the day,
nobody used the phrase *back in the day*.
So before its invention, what on earth did we say?
perhaps back then or maybe in my day.

The time referred to by this phrase
seems to depend on the speaker's age.
It's often a time we remember fondly
like we're turning back to an earlier page.

I've looked up its origin, on Google of course,
to see what they have to say.
"It came out of rap in the 1980s"
In other words back in the day.

Screwfix and Toolstation

I've been getting worrying emails
in my inbox recently.
How have these people found me?
by phishing, probably.

I'm trying not to open them
in case they're nasty scams
tempting me to visit
dodgy sites run by Madames.

Should I click or should I not?
I could just bin them now,
but I did that twice the other week,
and they're back again somehow.

Perhaps if I dare to open them
I can choose to unsubscribe,
but I might see things I shouldn't see
as a man of seventy-five.

Oh well, here goes, I'll take my chance
and choose a site to click on.
Screwfix? Toolstation? Which should it be?
I don't know which to pick on.

I tossed a coin to choose the site -
it landed for Toolstation.
The email opened easily -
it was quite a revelation!

Twenty percent off lawnmowers
Was the thing that caught my eye.
They were offering me a trade discount
for everything D-I-Y.

"Phew!" I went "Thank God for that!"
So I opened Screwfix next:
"Spring Into Action and get your work done"
Did they think I was oversexed?

No! Masonry paint and Water pumps,
Everything for Gardens -
another harmless D-I-Y site
offering jolly useful bargains.

Wheat field

How would Hockney paint this field?
He might start with a band of sky blue,
dotted with titanium white,
then green grain heads of wheat
floating horizontal in the breeze.
Delicate shimmering fibres,
paying homage to the sun.

Below that, the cobalt-teal stalks
supporting the proud heads of wheat,
standing stiff as the local militia,
firm roots instead of feet,
then a thin strip of terracotta
edging the field, protecting the crop,
and last, an emerald band.

Of course Hockney, with his enigmatic smile,
uses paint not these flat words.

Indoor gardening

It's been a long cold winter.
The trees are still quite bare,
but the grass is growing longer
as is my lockdown hair.

We've got a couple of indoor plants
of sadly stunted growth;
it's because we never water them,
our fault is sinful sloth.

But there's another kind of house plant
that will not be ignored;
it's an insistent little creeper
that may yet win an award.

It grows outside, but visits us
through a skylight it creeps in;
it dangles down beside our fridge
and ends by the rubbish bin.

Our ailments

When you get to be a certain age -
it tends to be your final stage -
an absorbing subject of conversation,
when you've finished discussing the state of the nation,
and describing what you had for lunch or dinner,
detailing your health is a certain winner.

You listen politely to your friends' grim descriptions,
their latest diagnoses, their repeat prescriptions.
They tell you about gall stones and aching joints
in their sad attempt to score extra points.
You shake your head, show fake concern,
waiting, 'cos soon it'll be your turn.

Yes, it's a contest. Didn't you know it?
Course you did, but you can't show it.
You may trump their aches with your operations,
you can show them your scars in hidden locations,
describe in detail your tonsilitis,
your covid symptoms, your conjunctivitis.

But you must know by now it's pointless trying
to outdo your friends, who are probably lying.
However interesting their ailments are
Yours are always more serious by far.

Footnote
I've just developed Tourette's I fear,
'cos every time I see or hear
a Tory on the television,
whose speech is met with clear derision,
to me he's the worst of enemies
So I scream at the screen foul obscenities.

Camelia

My camelia grows awkwardly
in its wooden demi-barrel -
its staves crooked and hoops loose,
its rivets broken and rusted.
It leans at forty-five degrees
distorted by age and weather.
Yet every Spring it blooms again -
with bright stunning crimson flowers
and only fades to brown in May.

Rainfall helps the staves revive
and tightens the hoops anew -
once more strong and healthy,
it stands straight for a month or two.

It's time, Good Sir

It's time, Good Sir, to pay something back
for your family's enslavement of men,
whose labour and lives brought you untold wealth,
obscene privilege now and then.

You claim you're not responsible
for your family's cruelty and greed.
You regret their dependence on slavery,
but will always be one of their breed.

Your thousands of English acres are encircled
By brick walls built centuries ago.
Do you ever wonder, in bed at night,
if these walls could protect you now?

The land your family cleared on Barbados
was a thriving sugar plantation,
worked by forced labour from Africa -
shameful mass black immigration.

The abolition of slavery reduced your sugar wealth,
but you were compensated handsomely
for your trouble and your loss.
The land has not been handed back - it still belongs to you!

Less than ten miles from your rural seat,
in your present country fiefdom,
is a village, where two centuries past,
working men fought for their very survival.

Those of your class sent six village men
to Tasmania and Botany Bay,
for daring to band together to fight for better pay.
These were God-fearing farmers, not criminals.

But the fuse had been lit, and the masses were moved
to demand the release of the Six.
And to avoid a French Revolution
they were pardoned and allowed to return.

Today we don't enslave men in quite the same way,
yet poverty still endures.
And the gap between you and poor country folk
is as wide as ever it was.

You and your kind survive by giving away just a little,
in order to prevent catastrophic unrest.
"Bread and circuses" some call it.
How long can you brave this farce out?

There are thirty-six food banks near your home.
Which of these would you choose to frequent
if the tables were turned and you lost everything,
and your family's blood funds were spent?

So, it's time, Good Sir, to pay something back -
perhaps your sugar plantation?
Return it to the Barbadian people
for the good of their newly-born nation.

Witch-hazel

Snapping alder, Winterbloom,
Wych elm, Tobacco wood,
they say witch hazel's bark and leaves
will cure all common ills.

Has flowers in winter, leaves in May,
we make Y-rods from its branches,
to find ground water, minerals
and other priceless treasures.

It must be magic, mustn't it?
No. This witch is not related
to broomstick crones, of either hue.
The root is wiche – to bend.

One day soon we may rely
on potent plants like these.
When man-made remedies fail to cure,
we'll go back to plants and trees.

Nailfile

Bugger it!
What?
I've dropped your nailfile
Pick it up then!
I can't.
Why not?
It's fallen between the floorboards.
Really – it's my best nailfile
Can't you reach it?
What, from between the floorboards?
Wherever.
I'll have a try.
No – can't reach it!   Oh bugger it!
Now what?
I've snagged my nail.
Serves you right.
Have you got a spare nailfile?
No.

On a ledge

We know we're living on a ledge.
It's dangerous and scary
in peril on the very edge,
we're permanently wary.

They rang the siren long ago
when we were sitting pretty,
relaxed and going with the flow,
snubbing their subcommittee.

When clouds appeared in a distant sky,
we took umbrellas with us.
We told ourselves they'd keep us dry
and wondered why the fuss.

Now as our ledge begins to crack,
we feel afraid, but can't go back.

The beautiful game

When people ask me "Who's your team?"
I tell them I don't have one.
They look at me in disbelief;
everyone has one, don't they?
Not me I say, I'm not a fan
of any club or league.
Football's a game for greedy men
Exploiters of fans and teams.

I think again and realize
that what I've said's not true -
I started following my local team in 1952.
It was Altrincham in the Cheshire League,
I remember my first match clearly.
It was against Hyde, a superior side.
My team were losing badly.

A boy my age standing next to me
said "Are you stickin' up for Hyde?"
I shyly shook my head and blushed
and very nearly cried.

When I was eight, we moved down south.
I watched matches with my granddad.
He'd played himself when he was young,
supported Man United.
In Surrey he followed his local team:
Redhill in the Athenian League.
We sat high in the stand, clapped our team,
had tea and crisps at half time.

My mum was a fan of United too,
so I kept an eye on them,
collected players' picture cards
from packs of bubble gum.
My hero was Duncan Edwards
of handsome Brylcreemed fame,
but the fifty-eight Munich air crash
killed him and my love of the game.

It was sparked again in the eighties
by a boys' team in Clacton-on-Sea,
when along with other parents
I watched my young son play.
Tom was a skilful player,
the midfield he patrolled,
always thought deeply about the game,
and scored the occasional goal.

Moving on

He worked for a multinational.
She was a community nurse.
He was moved to Maidenhead.
She refused to budge.

He earned more than she did.
She was more content.
He moved out in August.
She kept the family home.

By chance there were no children.
They went their separate ways.
He wished her well. She waved him off.
Both moved to happier days.

Flags and photos

Some people choose golden stars
to festoon their social media.
Others display allegiances
via their page on Wikipedia

But if you're a British minister,
you do not have this choice;
you're forced to plant a Union Jack
behind you when you voice

the official line on the BBC,
that patriotic cosh,
with frame-loads of photos of the queen
our screens are now awash.

And woe-betide you if you grin
when observing this charade.
If you're a presenter on TV,
better keep a straight facade.

Lawn damage

A mound of soft and sandy soil
has erupted on my lawn,
blighting my perfect Eden
an excrescence newly born.

I kicked it with my heavy boot.
It instantly came alive
with alien, red-brown life forms,
fleeing to survive.

Scurrying in all directions,
driven from their tranquil rest,
some of them salvaged tiny eggs
from their crumbling Kabul nest.

Amazon

Amazon is a simple synonym
for the mindless vandalism
of greedy men who give not a damn
for romantic idealism.

Maybe you see the rainforest
being cleared for grazing land
for cattle to feed our beeflust
when meat-eating's all but banned.

Or maybe you think of the mindless waste
dumped by that online store
who stack'em high and sell'em cheap
or fly-tip'em: Amazon whore.

Connections

Shall I tell you why the roads
are so cluttered in the mornings?
It's cos parents drive their kids to school
despite environmental warnings.

In years gone by, kids walked to school
or went there on their bikes.
Others went by bus or train.
What was there not to like?

I ran a mile to catch a bus
which took me to a station.
And unless unlucky, I got there
in time for my connection.

I got off thirty minutes later
at a busy London junction,
and travelled another seven miles
if I caught my next connection.

My final station left me
just a short walk from my school.
My journey had taken an hour and a half!
Today they'd think that cruel!

The great Aussie deal

We'll have lamb and beef and sugar
at tariff-free low prices -
things we should be eating less of
to avoid health-related crises.

How will they send this stuff to us
from ten thousand miles away?
Will the carcasses travel by sea or air?
or in a more nature-friendly way?

Do we really need this extra food?
We already grow it here.
Our farmers are now complaining
their markets could soon disappear.

But every trade deal has two sides -
we'll be selling our goods down under:
whisky, cars and biscuits, but
doesn't it make you wonder?

Are we encouraging drink driving
or putting Aussies out of jobs?
What kind of biscuits will we send
Garibaldis or Hob Nobs?

Will our fate as global Britons hang
on such neo-colonial trade?
On more post-Brexit waffling
By the Johnson-Truss brigade?

Rook society

There's an old country saying
that goes something like this:
If you see one rook, it's a crow;
If you see a flock of crows, they're rooks.

We had a flock of noisy rooks
in our tulip tree today,
making such a racket.
What were they trying to say?

Turned out there was a young rook,
you could hear its pitiful cry,
on its first outing from the nest,
it was learning how to fly

Its parents, brothers and sisters
watched over its flapping wings.
neighbours screeching, starlings shrieking
to save it from arrows and slings.

The rookie took off and reached a wall.
Its audience observed protectively.
Who was it said, some time ago
"There's no such thing as society?"

Deadheading

Deadheading's a job for your parents
when they've nothing better to do,
hoping to prolong the life of the plant,
making it bloom anew.

It gives them a new lease of life,
Mother said, "You should deadhead, too
You and the plant will live longer."
I thought "What a daft thing to do!"

But when you reach a certain age,
deadheading works - it's true!
Then you realise you're the age your parents were
when they suggested deadheading to you.

Normality

Despite what many people say
there's no such thing as normalité.
It may be hard to explain away
our myriad abnormalités

People like to think they're normal,
but they are actually ultra-conformal.
They may look down on others as "other"
not their sister or their brother.

So what on earth can we do about this?
Just avoid those who take the piss?
I say reject the norms! Refuse to bend!
to the latest fashion, the current trend.

No one's born normal – it's thrust upon us
by parents and friends and those who love us.
They earnestly think they're doing us a favour,
but why do we need an external saviour?

So, when we realise we're not one of the herd,
It comes as a shock – our senses are blurred.
We struggle against a lifetime's illusion,
which turns out to be just a empty delusion.

Footnote
I'm not really sure I'd agree with Larkin:
that grumpy old poet was clearly barkin'.
Misogynist git who blamed all parents
for fuckin' up their adolescents.

Up a bit

Up a bit. No, not that far.
Yes, that's it, now left a bit.
No - your left, not mine.
A bit further.
Yeah - just there.
Be gentle - not so hard
That's better.
Now down a bit.
And slower.
Arrgh! – that's lovely.

But if a friend is not around,
just do it for yourself,
up against a door frame,
or on a handy kitchen shelf.

The ballad of Shamima Begum

A teenage girl from Bethnal Green
with Bangladeshi roots,
her name's Shamima Begum.
She's the subject of disputes.

We saw her leaving Gatwick
with two friends veiled in black.
Those images still haunt us.
Why should we take her back?

She paid for flights with money
she stole from Mum and Dad.
Took a passport from her sister
for her journey to jihad

All the way to Syria
to join the Caliphate.
Only fifteen, for God's sake
too young to procreate.

She'd watched breath-taking footage
of young men wielding knives,
beheading western captives:
revenge for Muslim lives.

Radicalised is a scary word;
we all fear stark extremes,
but the videos Shamima saw
inspired her teenage dreams.

So different from the crap she'd watched
so often on TV.
so much more real than Hollyoaks
or the news on the BBC.

To the brothers of Islamic State
she might have been a spy,
sent there to gain intelligence,
to infiltrate and pry.

But days after her arrival
there was a man for her to wed.
They had two children hastily:
fighters for the cause were bred

At first her life was normal there,
an earnest ISIS bride,
recruiting women for jihad,
but her own two children died.

She knew of executions there.
She witnessed many sins,
and vowed it didn't faze her
seeing severed heads in bins.

She became a strict enforcer
of ISIL's moral laws.
She inspected clothes the women wore,
Worked daily for the cause.

She'd stitch a bomber in a vest -
that cruel death device,
to blow him and his enemies up
on his path to paradise.

The friends Shamima travelled with
all went their separate ways.
She later found they'd perished
in western bombing raids.

When at last Shamima saw
the evil ISIS way,
killing and torturing innocents
she took flight and ran away.

She fled from Raqqa pregnant,
to escape the Caliphate,
with a third child on the way so soon
she faced a tragic fate.

The Kurdish camp she fled to
was another hell on earth,
no place to raise a little child,
no place for giving birth.

Talking to her mother here,
she pleaded to come back
to save her new-born baby,
prepared to face the flack.

But for us she was a terrorist.
We would not let her in.
We took away her human rights,
would not forgive her sin.

We wouldn't go to rescue her,
To plead her case at home.
Her baby boy was born, but died,
now she's stateless and alone.

But why have we abandoned her,
denied a second chance
to a child who dreamt of a different world?
Why do we take this stance?

Is it because the cause she chose
is the anithesis of ours?
Do we really fear what she might do?
Does she have real evil powers?

Is it because she married young
then let three children die?
Or is it because she's brown not white
and now too damaged to cry?

Her lack of tears, confirms our fears,
so we're leaving her to rot,
stateless in a foreign land,
soon to be forgot.

Amberlist

I've planned my trip to Amberlist,
I've booked my Air B & B,
I'll be flying Budget Airlines,
I'll be spreading my bonhomie.

Happy days in those sunny uplands,
no distancing or wearing a mask,
I'll be supporting the local economy.
I've had the vaccine, so don't even ask.

I'm chilling out on Amberlist beach,
I'm sampling their food and their drink.
They say squid is good at this time of year
washed down with prosecco that's pink.

I'm spending my money freely,
nourishing my cultural brain.
I'm passing my nights with local girls,
sharing my Deltastrain.

I'll be making my way back home again
when all my money's spent.
I'll make quite sure they don't quarantine me.
That's a rule I'll circumvent.

When I bid farewell to you, Amberlist,
I'll shed a happy tear.
And if you all survive my trip,
I'll be sure to return next year.

(added Sept 21)
But hang on a mo, what's that I hear -
Amberlist has ceased to be?
How can that happen to my favourite resort?
Now where shall I go to be free.

Virus vocabulary

The virus has given birth
to some great new language usage.
Linguists are having a field day
R-Number, Herd Immunity,
Asymptomatic, Ventilator
Social Distancing and Respirator
Working-from-home and Covid 19
Self-Isolation and Quarantine.

But as well as these, there's a new-born verb
which is frequently spoken and frequently heard.
It's usable, it seems, in every tense,
and makes all too obvious common sense.
At first two words, often collocated,
then after a while it was hyphenated.
When you hear what it is, you'll understand why
everyone's now using to *sadlydie*.

As I walked out...

As I walked out one May morning
to take the pleasant air,
to Westminster I chanced to stray
and espied a damsel fair.

I stepped up to this charming maid
and askèd for her name
"Carrie is my name," she said.
"And 'tis my wedding day."

"Who is the lucky man?" probed I.
"One Boris," she did say.
He labours round these parts at times,
and married we shall be.

These names they rang a bell with me,
they were a famous pair.
This day they were to marry.
What day could be more fair?

The news next day came loud and shrill:
"Boris and Carrie Marry"
Sadly I misheard this news
As "Boris commits Hari-Kari."

Waiting for an Indian take-away

They're busy tonight, but it won't be long.
>   *Did they say how long?*
'bout ten minutes. Have a papadum to keep you going.
>   *It doesn't take ten minutes to eat a poppadom*
Don't eat it then.
>   *And do what with it?*
Be creative. Make something out of it.
>   *Like what?*
Break it into three pieces.
>   *And?*
Look - that piece could be Brittany.
>   *Oh yeah - and this bit's Australia without Tasmania.*
Great! Just five minutes left. Now how about the Greek
archipelago?
>   *Tricky.*
Not really - just crumble it and scatter the bits on that blue plate.
>   *Okay.*
Oh look! Here's our meal. Let's go.
>   *Ok – when I've eaten my papadum.*

Poppies red, white or black

We wear poppies in remembrance of those who have died
fighting for their countries in wars worldwide.
Soldiers and their officers on perilous missions
sent out to fight by politicians,
who need to quench their macho pride
by proving themselves the stronger side.
Wearing poppies demands that all wars cease.
Red, white or black - all stand for peace.

Poppies recall and keep clear in our mind
the limbless, the gassed, the maimed and the blind,
the shell-shocked young men who were shot for desertion,
or patched up and sent back – it was brutal coercion.
And others who suffered because of the war,
children evacuated but not all cared for,
blameless aliens behind enemy lines,
put behind bars though not guilty of crimes,
conscientious objectors who refused to fight,
despised for claiming their human right.

Our poppies demand that all wars cease.
Red, white or black - all stand for peace.

Pests

Slugs have nibbled our bean plants,
covered them with their slime.
They've crawled in like thieves and snacked on the leaves.
We're defenceless against their crime.

Snails have gnawed our petunias,
wrecked them without pity or care,
a few bits left hanging, limp petals dangling,
their stems violated and bare.

Blue tits have pecked our sweet peas,
demolished each pale, fragrant bloom.
Their tendrils still cling to the trellis, like springs.
They're confronting their untimely doom.

The government's starved local councils,
flogged off houses and privatised health,
academized schools with despotic rules.
to add to their cronies' gross wealth.

Granddaughter

Ivy's holding a baby
tenderly.

She's gazing at the baby
lovingly.

Ivy's seven, I'm seventy-five,
and a bit doddery.

Ivy will be holding her own baby,
eventually.

I'll see them together,
hopefully.

Ivy's seven, I'm seventy-five
and a bit doddery.

Unclear about nuclear

Back in the day they called it M A D -
Mutually Assured Destruction,
perversely a way of maintaining the peace,
keeping missiles in overproduction.
But in the end, what's the point of nuclear
as a means of defence or attack?
It's bonkers to think we could win a war
without getting caught up in the flak.

But...
Now we're helping our Aussie chums
to build nuclear submarines.
They're planning to strut the Pacific stage
in these evil killing machines.
Will they dare to threaten China
before China hits back at them?
Do they dream they can win an unwinnable war
while avoiding the fallout phlegm?

And...
As if this wasn't bad enough,
the USA's also onboard
to provide toxic Trumpian terror -
an atomically-armed warlord.
Two catastrophes now seem on the cards:
climate change and nuclear conflict.
If one doesn't get you, the other one will
So choose!

Which one have you picked?

Wounded

I was trying to defend Joseph
To protect him from David.
They were real arrows
with sharp metal tips.

I stood between David and Joseph,
not expecting him to shoot,
but David was very angry
And drew back the bow string.

I stood there defiant.
Joseph began to cry.
David took aim and fired.
The arrow pierced my thigh.

I pulled it out slowly.
It left a small hole,
which I covered with a plaster.
When my parents asked, I didn't tell.

The pain got worse and I had to admit
what had happened that Sunday morning.
The wound healed very quickly
Leaving just a small, round scar.

That happened seventy years ago -
It seems like yesterday.
But I looked at my thigh this morning
The scar and memory are clear.

Yap yap yap

What're you doing about inequality -
you know, the gap between rich and poor?
There are more and ever more homeless;
even food banks are running short.

> *We're investing more in yap yap yap.*
> *Wages are going up yap yap yap.*
> *There's plenty of well-paid yap yap yaps.*
> *Our new hard shit fund will yap yap yap.*

And what're you doing about shortages
of drivers and doctors and carers,
who keep us all supplied and safe
with fuel and food and welfare?

> *We're not shying away from yap yap yap.*
> *We're taking full responsa...yap yap yap.*
> *We're issuing visas for yap yap yap.*
> *And training our troops to yap yap yap.*

And how about saving the planet
from the threat of climate change?
You know – melting ice and heatwaves
floods and things like that?

> *There's a conference soon in yap yap yap*
> *Global leaders will yap yap yap*
> *Our world-beating know-how will yap yap yap*
> *And solve every yap yap yap.*

And don't forget the embattled police,
the force you cut to the bone,
so much so they've had to employ
abusers, sex- and ex-offenders

> *Look! Not all the police are yap yap yap.*
> *They're a committed team of yap yap yap,*
> *who are doing their level yap yap ... ...*

Scum

It's an impolite word, I have to admit,
but in the context it's surely apt,
to describe those entitled bullies
who crush us and leave us trapped.

They take money from the pockets
of the poor and dispossessed.
They take food from the mouths of children,
their families and the rest.

They leave streets strewn with homeless bodies,
who've fallen on wretched times.
They refuse them shelter and nourishment,
and fine them for petty crimes.

They spread scorn for asylum seekers,
wishing them into the waves,
branding them scroungers and spongers,
abusing these modern-day slaves.

So don't be so faux-offended
by the use of that four-letter term.
Considering who it's aimed at,
scum seems mild for this sleazy firm.

What does it mean?

If you understand a poem,
does it mean it's mediocre?
And if you don't,
does it mean you're dim?

I like the sound of poems
and their appearance on a page,
but some of them elude me -
their significance, I mean.

I'm writing poems now myself.
It's easier that way.
At least I understand them,
and I hope that others may.

About the author

When he was about 7, Simon Haines went in for a national poetry competition for primary school children and, to his amazement, won second prize. The competition asked children to write an extra verse to the nursery rhyme *Old Mother Hubbard*. Simon was too shy to go to London to collect the prize, and sadly he didn't keep that extra verse as proof of his early promise.

He has always written poems and songs though few have seen the light of day until now. Lockdown gave him more time to write and more subjects to write about. Several of his poems have been included on the Poetry Wivenhoe Lockdown collection website, and two of these were included in their printed collection **Tales Told By Birds**. Other poems have been broadcast on BBC Radio Essex. His first collection of poems, **Sea Planes and Seed Trays**, was published in 2019.

In addition to poems and songs, Simon has written many English language textbooks for speakers of other languages as well as articles for folk music magazines.

In his spare time, Simon plays music in three groups: *Bof!*, *Rosewood* and *The Hosepipe Band*, a group which plays for ceilidhs and accompanies poetry readings by Martin Newell and Blake Morrison.

Contact: *simonhaines1@icloud.com*

Sea Planes and Seed Trays

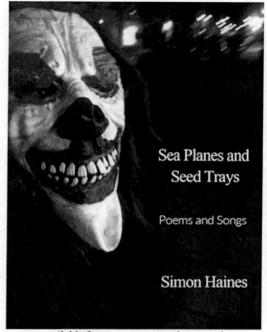

Sea Planes and
Seed Trays

Poems and Songs

Simon Haines

available from *www.rosewoodpress.co.uk*

Review by Terence Blacker

The cover illustration of Simon Haines's poetry collection SEA PLANES AND SEED TRAYS has a gruesome look. It is of a grotesque, yellow-toothed masked figure which would not be out of place at voodoo party on the streets of New Orleans.

Don't be fooled. The poems and songs in this book are approachable and funny, capturing the joys and pains of everyday life with real warmth and poignancy. When there is justified anger and frustration at the world outside, it is of the ironic, low-key kind - and all the more effective for that.

The poem which gives the book its title captures a conversation, full of misunderstandings and affectionate exasperation, between the poet and his granddaughter.

> *'My granddaughter said in a serious tone*
> *As she painted a unicorn pink*
> *For no actual reason I could discern*
> *We're learning about sea planes this week.*
> *Sea planes? I queries sounding slightly surprised*
> *My! The curriculum has broadened out!'*

And so the trail inter-generational misconnection begins.

'Sea Planes and Seed Trays' sets the tone of the collection. This is family life as we all can recognise it. But Simon Haines is also politically aware and, between the lines of these poems and songs, there are thoughts of a darker, crueler world outside - a world of racism, poverty, division, unfairness, an under-funded NHS, and heartless, self-serving government.

The best poems here reflect the collision between this brutal, chilly outside world and our own pampered existence. With a wry self-awareness of the writer's personal helplessness in the face of global disaster, **'Climate Emergency'** opens with the words:

> *'When the drought in Africa hit the news,*
> *I made an ethical choice*
> *Every time I cleaned my teeth*
> *I turned the cold tap off.'*

ISBN 978-1-7398759-0-9